Life 101

A NEW VISIONARY UNDERSTANDING OF CHRISTIAN FULFILMENT

Dr. Ngonde Ajah Thomas

Copyright © 2014 by Dr.Ngonde Ajah Thomas

LIFE 101
A New Visionary Understanding of Christian Fulfilment.
by Dr.Ngonde Ajah Thomas

Printed in the United States of America

ISBN 9781629524320

All rights reserved solely by the author. The author guarantees all contents are original and do not infringe upon the legal rights of any other person or work. No part of this book may be reproduced in any form without the permission of the author. The views expressed in this book are not necessarily those of the publisher.

Scripture quotations taken from the King James Version (KJV) – public domain

Scripture quotations taken from the New International Version (NIV). Copyright © 1973, 1978, 1984, 2011 by Biblica, Inc.™. Used by permission. All rights reserved.

www.xulonpress.com

Preface

I had just updated my status on facebook with an inspirational statement as was my custom since becoming an active user of this social handle. This is what I wrote: "the eyes are meant for vision not judgment; allow your heart to judge while the eyes stick to their role...we get more trouble switching these roles!". A series of laudatory and affirmative comments ensued. One of the comments read thus: "Doc you be na Prof oh…" which is Cameroonian pidgin-English for: "Doc you are a Professor". I laughed and jokingly replied: "surely a professor of life and the course is called life 101". That is how this book got its title. Compassion for my fellow man and the wish to see everyone live happily has always been part of me. My life experiences growing up and my career of physician made this all the more obvious as I encountered people from all walks of life trying to put up with various challenges. Whether it was a physical problem or social problem, I was always ready to give what I had; be it skill, substance or soulful advice to help people out of the troubles they faced. When I made a decision to get to know God even better in July 2011 the spectrum of help I could offer extended into the spiritual. I would pray for people and they would experience positive changes in their lives. I'd study the word of God and gain revelations that I'd share with my friends in person and on facebook. Over time, my urge to help people live fulfilled lives in Christ Jesus increased and seeing the feedback I got, I dared to go the extra mile of crystallizing my thoughts into this book so that a wider audience could be edified. Written between the months of February 2013 through December 2013, this book is a product of sacrifice, prayer, and careful bible studies. Joggling my job of Peace Corps Medical Officer and other family and social issues I managed to squeeze time after my morning prayers on most days to type out a little material before rushing to work. All scripture in this book was culled from the King James Version of the Holy Bible. Five years ago, a friend offered me award-winning teacher, Hal Urban's book entitled *Life's Greatest Lessons: 20 Things That Matter*; this book left me with a lasting impression-one that contributed in the realization of this work.

Life 101: A New Visionary Understanding of Christian Fulfillment contains a plethora of original concepts on the human experience of spirituality and on wisdom for life based on revelatory knowledge from the teachings of Jesus Christ on the Kingdom of God. Answering questions like; *is a "life education" necessary?* , *What constitutes my being?* , *Why am I here?*, this book ventures into some of the most pre-occupying issues the human has grappled with down the ages. At a time when our world seems to be even more hurting, and fulfilling one's purpose seems a distant mirage in this contemporary socio-economic and geo-political dispensation, this carefully knitted piece of work will offer any open-minded reader a panacea of hope, an anchor of faith and a roadmap to fulfilling their God-given purpose. It stresses all along the invaluable place of a closer relationship with our creator as the fundamental step to achieving success in life. The book is divided into ten chapters with a bullet-style summary at the end of the longer chapters. These bullet points can be used for further discussion. There is a summary for the entire book at the end with an acronym for easy retention. Have a pleasant read!

Ngonde Ajah Thomas, MD
500 Fairnest Court
Dover DE 19904
March 6, 2014

Dedication

To all peoples of the world who lack access to effective healthcare, especially the rural dwellers of my nation Cameroon.

Acknowledgement

I give all glory to God Almighty for giving me the inspiration to come up with this piece of work. Lord you are my strength and my shield.

Pastor Che Joseph: without your support in the proof-reading and scriptural correlation of the text, this book would not have been produced. Thank you very much brother.

To Pastors Nyentibenem Agbor, Hilda Catherine Kroon and Okesack Thompson: thank you all for helping me kick-start a spirit-led life and for continuously encouraging me in the Lord.

To my loving family: Daddy, Mama, Shushu, Papa, Mams, Emuks, Mercy, uncle Ekiti, Ernest, Divine and Etah, I am grateful for your unparalleled support towards the realization of this project. I love you all with my breath.

To Mr. Bruno Ayang my brother-in-law: Thanks for taking me into your house in Dover where I stayed to follow through the publishing of this book. Your brotherly love and warmth graced my stay. To you Toks and little Jayden, do not think I took for granted those playful moments we shared. Cheers!

To my friends: Dr.Gerald Nkafu, Roland Etamanyi, Mfotabi Eyisab, Ivo Pufong, Ela Ngambele Eboa, Valerie Esselle, Folefac Michael, Hilary Aben and Dr. Ojong Samuel: Thanks for believing that this dream I shared with you could become reality. To Fritz Nkongho, I can't forget your role in getting production work on my manuscript started. To you Lessly Bonam, Samuel Molombe and Esona Marie: your prayers and prophecies were an encouragement.To Nana Richard, Tanyi Ayuk, Melvis, Danielle, Catherine, Corantine, Ngang Lionel, Janvier,Vanessa, Lyse and all my other friends who gave me moral support, thank you all.

Finally, I thank the whole Xulon Press crew for making me a published author.

Table of Contents

Preface v
Dedication. ix
Acknowledgement xi

Chapter I: Is A "Life Education" Necessary? . . . 15
Chapter II: The Mechanism And Merits
              of a Spiritual Re-Birth 22
Chapter III: What Constitutes My Being?. 34
Chapter IV: Why Am I Here? 52
Chapter V: What Is My Area Of Stewardship? . . 58
Chapter VI: Open Up The Limits 67
Chapter VII: Run With The Vision 71
Chapter VIII: Effort Alone Is Insufficient...
              Faith Is A Must! 77
Chapter IX: Communicate Adequately
              and Wisely 83

Chapter X: Relax...Shine A Smile! 90

Summary 95

CHAPTER I

Is A "Life Education" Necessary?

It is a widely acclaimed view that education is the most powerful weapon to bring about positive change in the world. While this theory is logical, as well as true to some extent, it leaves much to be desired. Illiteracy has long been linked to several problems the world suffers today, but the increase in knowledge that has occurred over several centuries has failed to erase, if not worsen, some of the problems our world faces. We are in the first quarter of the 21st century, in the heart of the dot.com phenomenon where the spread of knowledge seems to be at its apogee, but our world is still beset by staggering statistics of social injustices, poverty, inter-cultural conflicts, civil wars and outright human right violations. The perpetrators of most of these deplorable injustices surely are not illiterates but educated men and women, people who were privileged to receive one of the finest classroom trainings! Despite being an important factor for human development, education is not all that it takes to achieve the true positive change our world craves. The more learned someone is doesn't necessarily make him a better world citizen. In fact, it could be argued that an educated man has the power to become more dangerous to society than an uneducated person!

Formal education and vocational training provide people with knowledge and skills that enable them to make a career and achieve financial independence and to 'enjoy life'. This seems to be the central goal for every toiling we see around. People tend to be absorbed with doing this thing or that thing in order to "make it in life". Sure, education is a critical promoter of human development and wellbeing both at an individual and collective level. Sad as it is however, education and her gains thereof are insufficient to guarantee fulfillment to the human soul! Education on life gets a little closer and the core course of 'Love education' works the miracle. It is only love and the relentless pursuit of it that can bring true fulfillment to the human soul and eclipse our world into a safe haven for everyone to live in. In schools, very little time and energy are committed (if at all provided) to teach people about life and love as a whole. The means and methods to improve our personalities so as to get the most out of life and be a blessing to the world around us does not feature in our curricula. Even religious settings that get a little close miss the whole point. They approach this topic like a lesson in arithmetic! Their approach is usually mentally-oriented with no recourse to a conscious and sincere change of heart. The result of this being a flimsy temporary effect with hardly any sustained practical benefit for the individual and the society.

This brings us to the purpose of this book, which is to challenge the reader's thought system on the topic of unconditional love as prescribed in the teachings of the greatest true lover ever-Jesus Christ of Nazareth. It seeks to provoke the reader's spirit and to unveil his or her ability to love unconditionally and so chart the course to his/her fulfillment.

As we can learn to read and write, so too can we learn to live life more effectively for our good and the good of the world. Like a raw material, the human being requires continue processing so as to obtain the best possible version of him/her. The first and most crucial machine in the processing factory is called Jesus Christ. He exhorted: *seek ye first the **kingdom of God** and its righteousness and all other things shall be added unto you.* While some people are caught up in the 'have-to' web of life I have to go to school, I have to get a job, I have to get married, I have to raise my kids) others are not even sure what Jesus meant in that verse. The ***Kingdom of God*** is not a place, but a system; a system engineered by the practice of unconditional love with the benefit of unlimited fulfillment that comes with it. The human is incomplete; he doesn't automatically experience fulfillment from birth. That's why he needs to seek the kingdom of God to become complete. The only way a human can experience the kingdom of God is through spiritual rebirth and a sustained fellowship with the Holy Spirit. Eternity is a characteristic feature of this system, the fulfillment that comes with it is eternal! The scriptures tell us that eternity is set in our hearts **(Ecc 3:11-NIV, John 11:24-25)**. The scripture also says the Kingdom of God is within us**(Luke 17:20-21)**,in other words, we have what it takes; we are all potentially capable of loving unconditionally and living a fulfilled life in this world and in the world beyond after we pass on. However, we must set a solid foundation. Is there any man who sets out to build a house without counting its cost? Jesus, the author of good success and fulfillment asked his followers some two thousand years ago. He challenged them with this rhetorical question with the aim of teaching them the first success lesson ever, planning! If we plan to live a fulfilled life, we must have recourse to the area of our beings that can guarantee this, our spirit.

Eternal fulfillment, righteousness, joy and peace **(Romans 14:17)**which represent the Kingdom of God, are all programmed within the human spirit. Paying frequent attention to your spirit will enable you to tap into this dimension of bliss despite the peril and turbulence of the world.

Pearls

- ✓ The source of our world's problems is not the lack of education but the absence of love and the absence of a "correct love education."
- ✓ Going to school, learning a trade, grabbing a good job are insufficient for a man to enjoy a fulfilled life.
- ✓ Down the ages, religion has failed and will continue to fail because it seeks to make people love unconditionally by educating their minds.
- ✓ Unconditional love is a spiritual ability and can only be imparted on the human spirit, a humbled and repentant one. It can never be learned by the mind(**Romans 5:17, Eph2:4-9, John 3:16, Is 1:19**)
- ✓ Every human soul thirsts for the kingdom of God without knowing.

- ✓ The Kingdom of God is not a place but a love system.
- ✓ This system of love and her benefits of eternal fulfillment are programmed in every human spirit.
- ✓ To unravel this system from within, a man must die to self.
- ✓ Dying to self means allowing Jesus Christ to recreate your human spirit through repentance and allowing love and the living word to rule your life as long as you live.
- ✓ Jesus Christ rules the life of every person who has died to self.
- ✓ Only the revelation of Christ in a human soul can enable them to treat each other right and guarantee their eternal fulfillment. Any education/preaching/teaching/philosophy/theology that falls short of recreating the human spirit is a mere mental exercise!

CHAPTER II

The Mechanism And Merits Of A Spiritual Re-Birth

The notion of being "born-again" is a critical element in the life of a Christian. It is the first step that transits a Christian's mentality from a selfish tendency to a selfless one. It is the rate-limiting step. It is pretty much like enabling a function in a computer software program. The function in this case is unconditional love! There's no human being that loves unconditionally unless he has had an encounter with Jesus Christ. This encounter doesn't have to be as spectacular as Saul's experience on the way to Damascus. It doesn't have to be a ceremony that is chaired by a minister of God. On the contrary; it is a thing of the heart. *Enter into thy closet...* Jesus admonished; in other words, look inwardly. Being born again happens in the twinkle of an eye. It is that moment when deep inside your heart, you acknowledge your sins, you are remorseful and you sincerely wish to not go back to the sins and then you recognize the sacrifice of Jesus as the only atonement for your guilt and ask him to take control hence forth. The only essential ingredients in this procedure are your sincerity and calling upon the name of Jesus Christ! Unfortunately, this concept is one of the most controversial Christianity has ever known. It has been misconstrued by many, misrepresented by some and out rightly scoffed by others. Yet it stands as the surest source of strength for the Christian. This is not surprising at all because the devil, who was defeated by Christ's sacrifice on the cross **(Col 2:13-15)**, will not allow Christians to unveil the treasures wrought for them by that divine sacrifice. It is the devil's desire that humans trod this world completely clueless of who they truly are, so they do not express let alone enjoy the benefits, the spoils of a battle fought and won for them 2000years ago. *He has blinded the eyes of men* **(2Cor 4:4)**.

Let's take a little walk in the Garden of Eden. Before the fall of man, we learn that Adam was given authority over every creature-this includes the "serpent", the devil. Adam lived in an atmosphere of total love without fear, shame or guilt of any sort. However, when he listened to the devil's voice and got influenced by it, which marked the beginning of confusion, doubt, fear and a tendency to sin for the human. He had just lost his authority to the devil...a terrible error that would haunt humankind till death unless he subscribes to the correction brought by the second Adam-Jesus(**1Cor 15:45**). Now, the devil could influence man's thoughts in whatever ways to suit his own intentions which are contrary to the will of God. No amount of strong will can deliver a man from this! It could take only God himself to shed divine blood so that everyone who believes, denouncing his evil ways, the authority of the devil, and succumbing to God's own authority will regain that lost authority(**2Cor10:4-6**). This way, there is a new birth under a new Adam, Jesus Christ(**2Cor 5:17**) where guilt is taken away(**Rom8:1-3**) and we stand blameless before God with access to the tree of life!(**Rev 2:7**). In this state, we are able to see this world as naked as it is, show love unconditionally, and read and understand the word of God easily. We can also recognize easily the devil's schemes and shun him very readily as we grow everyday in the knowledge and practice of the word of God (**James 1:22-25**). Someone who has not achieved this new birth finds it hard to study, let alone understand, the word of God(**1Cor2:14-15**). It has been referred to by some as a 2000page sleep pill! The devil doesn't allow them to uncover the truth inherent in God's word. He has blinded their eyes(**2Cor4:4**).But when they do meet Christ, scales come off their eyes(spiritually) as it did physically with Saul who became Paul. Jesus further enlightens us on the preciousness of this gift of salvation by recounting a parable of a man who found treasure on a piece of land and ran back to sell all his property and use the money to buy that piece of land. That is what happens when we get an encounter with Jesus Christ; it is something we would never want to lose and can give up the world for, because there is nothing in this whole wide world we would ever compare to its sweetness, truth and peace. Explaining this to someone else may not reflect the real extent of what one feels. No wonder the psalmist recommends that we taste and see that the Lord is good(**Psalm 34:8**). If you do not taste, you will never have an iota of an idea of what goodness pertains to it–and the choice is yours. Salvation is available by the grace of God but without faith(obedience/humility), we can never ever receive it(**Eph 2:8**)! He says it's for children; meaning humble people, "foolish" people. He says... *it's easier for a camel to go through an eye of a needle than for a rich man to enter the Kingdom of God*...rich man here is the self-sufficient, the know-it-alls, the one who wants to reason everything about God...you do not reason God, you believe God because HE is God! Jesus did not perform a single miracle in his hometown because of the people's unbelief! What can a carpenter's son teach us, they probably wondered?

Christianity is a spiritual enterprise: only faith which is a spiritual function can purchase us anything. Faith is the only thing that pleases God, remember(**Heb11:6**)? No doubt Jesus Christ is the author and finisher of our faith (**Heb12:2**). He is the way, the truth and the life, the only way!

A humble yet timid Pharisee by name Nicodemus came to Jesus one night. He had seen Jesus teach with great wisdom, share and love with much passion, heal the sick and set free the demon-possessed. This was so remarkable that he was very certain that there was something special about Jesus-that he came from above. Simply put, he saw the kingdom of God at work in Jesus' life-so it is in our day. There are people who have unlocked the treasures of the Kingdom of God and operate is this system daily. It leaves some in dismay, some just scoff cynically, others are humble enough to realize that there is something good, something special, something wonderful about these people and are willing to learn and live that way. Like Nicodemus, these ones have an open heart, others are more courageous than Nicodemus; either ways they both get what they seek as the person points them to the master-Jesus Christ. Jesus first of all challenged Nicodemus who was a master of the law and could not comprehend the kingdom of

God. He was simply trying to point out here that no level of human accolades or investment to understand God count for anything. He told him you must be born again. No amount of man-made philosophy can afford one the ability to love unconditionally. They are strictly a mental exercise, fruitless to the human spirit! Being born again on the other hand has a direct spiritual effect because it inspires obedience to the word of God which has the ability to bring true change in the heart of man **(Ez36:26-27)**.

Jesus answered Nicodemus: *unless a man is born again, he cannot see the kingdom of God...Unless a man is born of water and the spirit, he cannot enter the kingdom of God*. Like explained above, being born again is like enabling a software program. If and when this is done, man is given the ability to love unconditionally, but he can choose to not do so. A man who is not born again can never love unconditionally, he does not understand it. That's why Jesus said he cannot "see" the kingdom; in other words it is happening all around him/her, but he/she has no clue; it flummoxes his/her understanding. Jesus did not end there; he said unless a man is born of water and the spirit, he cannot "enter" the kingdom of God. This now entails motion. It is not enough to become born again; you must walk in the light of God's word allowing it to rule your heart before unconditional love and true fulfillment can become part and parcel of you. So there are born-again Christians who can't still love others unconditionally, their lives are peace-starved, joy-starved and they are still vain and bitter. These are the type that see the kingdom but cannot enter it. They have the ability to love unconditionally but choose to not do so. But when a man both sees and enters the kingdom of God, the world feels it; they are prodigies, an enigma that some are jealous of, others remain indifferent and others come close to them to understand how this happened to them and to learn. Jesus continued explaining. *The wind bloweth where it listeth, and thou hearest the sound thereof, but canst not tell whence it cometh and whither it goeth: so is everyone born of the Spirit* (**John 3:8**). You can't comprehend the ways of someone born of the spirit; unconditional love becomes breathing for him/her; peace and joy never elude him/her, his/her courage frightens many, he has everything and gives everything!(**2Pet1:3-4, Rev 5:10, Romans 8:16-17, Gal 5:22-23**).

With our new spiritual identity, we are made perfect in Christ; this means we have become a "brand", a "kind" that God sees as Jesus Christ anytime he looks at us. Of course, this dispensation doesn't imply one who has unveiled the treasures of God's kingdom can never err. With respect to our behavior in the face of different temptations and challenges, perfection is a process; a process of persistence and insistence, the readiness to get back up each time we fall.(**Proverbs 24:16-18, 1John1:7, 1John 1:9**)

Pearls
- ✓ Without a spiritual rebirth, you can never be fulfilled in this world!
- ✓ Be sincere in your thoughts, be remorseful of your wrong deeds and ask Jesus Christ to take

control-the moment you do this you are born again-congratulations!

- ✓ Being born again is the first step to enjoying eternal fulfillment. Putting the word of God into practice sustains this fulfillment.
- ✓ Humility is the key-step to unlocking the kingdom of God.
- ✓ The human being has no love of his own (**Jer17:19**), there is nothing genuine in his love unless he comes in contact with true love, Jesus Christ (**Romans5:5**) Then can he reflect unto others the love imparted to him by Christ(**2Cor3:15-18**).
- ✓ A human being who has not met Christ is unable to love unconditionally even if he tries to...the one who has met Him is able but can choose to not do so!
- ✓ The human being is like raw material. He/she needs to be processed constantly to obtain a better version of him/her. The machine responsible for

this processing is called Jesus Christ, who is the living word of God **(Romans12:2)**!

✓ Building our lives on Christ helps shape our attitudes and empowers us to get the most out of life while making the world a better place for others to live in.

✓ The life of Jesus Christ is rich with winning strategies that can afford our personalities the highest possible efficiency.

✓ The mind can never comprehend unconditional love-it is a spiritual function.

✓ No amount of lessons in philosophy or theology can change a man. Let his spirit be broken first, and then can he understand unconditional love.

✓ The Kingdom of God is not a place but a system. It is a system engineered by the practice of unconditional love with an eternal benefit of limitless fulfillment attached to it.

✓ Philosophy and Theology are fruitless to the human spirit! They are basic mental exercises and can never open the treasures of the Kingdom of God to any person.

✓ Righteousness is the ability to love unconditionally.
✓ Like a gift, righteousness is imparted by grace to all those with a humble and repentant heart.

CHAPTER III

What Constitutes My Being?

If we understand our composition and the roles the different features play, we can live much more effectively and become much happier beings. The human being is made up of three main structures: spirit, soul and body. The body is the obvious part of our being while the soul and spirit constitute our inner being and are invisible. The soul is like an unstable chemical. It can operate in two different modes—the mental mode(mind) where reason and pleasure are primary and in the spiritual mode(spirit), where faith is the main mode of operation.

Our body is like a computer screen; it is endowed with the five senses: sight, audition, taste, touch and smell. These senses enable us to relate with the external environment and serve as a source of information to our second dimension, the soul, which hosts the mind. The mind is like the central processing unit (CPU) of our being. It receives information emanating from the senses and builds thoughts that ultimately define what we say and how we act-basically our attitude towards various situations. There is some bad news to this; just like the CPU of the computer, what we allow into our minds repeatedly is what we deliver through our character. We tend to become what we think –we are therefore made or marred by our minds. *As a man thinketh in his heart, so is he*...**(Proverbs23:7).**

It is therefore a good personal policy to watch what we let into our minds. This takes us to the good news of the story; we have the ability to choose what we let into our minds. Our choice is what charts the course of our life; like a train, it takes us to our various destinations in life: prosperity, failure, joy, bitterness, success, poverty, regrets. With the wrong choices, the mind could be an eternal prison, a source of self-inflicted pain and even death! As followers of Christ, the mind is that dimension of our being where the devil has access. It is like a battlefield between the devil and us. Paul had this revelation when he said in 2Cor10:4 *for the weapons of our warfare are not carnal, but mighty through God to the pulling down of strongholds.* The devil influences and sets us off-track of God's will, giving us reasons and mostly logical ones. A build up of thoughts derived from knowledge, emotions or memories that resists the truth of God's word in our heart is what the bible refers to as strongholds. Remember that the devil likes logic (refer to Eve's conversation with the serpent in the Garden of Eden). By the nature of Adam that all humans share, it is hard to win him at this level and to make the right choices regarding God's will. That's why God tricked him by sacrificing HIS only son...so that whosoever believes in him shall be saved...saved from what? From mental slavery! That through the power of the Holy Spirit, we shall be liberated and be poised to discern God's will, escaping all confusions the devil feeds our minds.

Mental slavery is what I define as **a subconscious erosion of one's personality or sense of self by service**

to a knowledge that does not guarantee true freedom. The mental slave is usually brainwashed by the philosophy of the system he or she serves and he exhibits one cardinal quality-fear. Fear of what may happen if he/she should quit or challenge the system which usually is his/her source of income. Fear of what people may talk about him/her if he stands out against the system (social disregard).Fear of the system itself which may be vicious enough to destroy him/her. Fear of what he/she may become because he is left with little or no personality to think for him after the system has claimed a toll of it. Oftentimes, a mental slave exhibits pride as well. Being brainwashed into believing his/her knowledge is superior and others who do not buy their idea are subordinate. While mental slavery could be incidentally or willfully perpetrated by a system or another individual, it can as well be self-imposed as in the case of strongholds above. In either case, there is usually an interconnection that weaves a complex web in the mind of the victim making it impermeable to the truth of God's word! Given the broadness of the topic of mental slavery, another book would contain a fuller elucidation it.

Our world is flooded with knowledge of all sort, most of which claim to set us free and give us a fulfilled life but in truth do not. Gradually, like a bricklayer's mold, we are fashioned in the image and likeness of such knowledge: science, traditions, academics, philosophies and others. Religion, sadly, also makes this list. As Ironic as this sounds, this is true. Religion is basically a human endeavor to please God. Religion does not guarantee us freedom, fulfillment or heaven but our personal relationship with God does! Religious leaders make their followers to believe (for selfish reasons or otherwise) that by obeying certain traditional principles, by carrying out certain rituals and offering certain sacrifices makes them acceptable to God. Only one sacrifice, shedding of divine blood, was enough-we do not need to make other sacrifices. The only sacrifice we owe God is that of our lives; living for him in holiness and as such living for others by loving them and untiringly putting into practice the word of God **(Romans 12:1).**

Those who allow the various human molds to control them usually believe reasonably or unreasonably that their mold is the most vital thing in life and nothing else really matters; they try to explain everything away including God, with a swipe of the hand using their learned principles. They develop a staunch attitude and refuse to yield to any idea that tries to suggest something different .The bible calls that a "yoke"; it is a yoke because it is burdensome and like an ox they carry it about miserably, yet proudly too! They never get satisfied with their knowledge and keep accumulating loads of it and their minds get narrower and narrower although they get an illusion of the opposite. The Holy Spirit through Paul, teaches us in Romans12:2 *And be not conformed to this world: but be ye transformed by the renewing of your mind, that ye may prove what is the good, and acceptable and perfect will of God.* In other words let no knowledge this world offers, take precedence over the guidance of God's word. Our minds must be renewed by the word of God which screens and frees us from any kind of mental slavery brought about by other types of knowledge. Not that gaining knowledge is a bad thing in itself, but the fact that people use their knowledge to supplant faith in God and bring Christ's sacrifice to naught is! It is only the living word of God, Christ himself who can model our minds to escape the negative effects these molds have on us and to determine the extent to which we can make use of them without compromising our faith in God. Paul put it nicely when he said in 2Cor10:5 *casting down imaginations, and every high thing that exalteth itself against the knowledge of God, and bringing into captivity every thought to the obedience of Christ.* This is further corroborated by; your word is a lamp for my path **(Psalm139:130, Psalm 139:105)** Christ is the light of life **(John 8:12)**.Isaiah prophesied our deliverance from mental slavery and other yokes placed by the manipulation of the devil when he said ...*on that day, his yoke shall be taken from off your neck, and his burden from off your shoulder and the yoke shall be broken because of the anointing***(Is 10:27)**. The anointing of God is the Holy Spirit, the power that works with every humble and repentant heart to effect the changes God brings about in their lives(**Acts 1:8**). Jesus himself made clear his role to overhaul the influences of the evil one on our lives when he launched his mission in **Luke4:18** *The spirit of the Lord is upon me and he has anointed me to bring glad tidings to the meek, healing to the broken hearted, set captives free, to set at liberty them that are bruised and to proclaim the acceptable year of the lord...* In one sentence, Christ summarized his mission on earth... take note that 'captives' represents human beings who are enslaved by whatever sleek devices or philosophies, which the devil uses to keep them in a shade. Only the leading of God's spirit can ensure control of the mind and give us victory every day and ultimately take us to our creator when we pass on. A quick step to diagnose our knowledge has gone wrong would be to ask ourselves these questions: is there a kind of knowledge I have acquired that renders me proud? Do other areas of my life suffer as a result of time spent gathering this knowledge? After all my years of grappling with this ideology, do I feel satisfied or do I feel I am missing something? Do I get angry anytime someone brings up an idea that is contrary to the ones I stand for? Do I have any fears regarding the knowledge I have acquired? Do I rely on this gained knowledge to explain away anything about God? Do I consider any other person who doesn't have my knowledge as inferior? Do I regard any other person who has not undergone my kind of training as unfit to say anything about God? Answering yes to one or a combination of these questions can quickly tell us we are carrying a yoke. We must come back to basics by studying and meditating on God's word which is the first knowledge, the knowledge of all knowledge, so that the Holy Spirit would inspire us and re-model our perspectives on the knowledge and influences this world offers us**(Romans12:2, 2Tim 3:16-17, Joshua1:8)**.

Best practices for the mind will be to use it wholly when it comes to working on a project, academics, innovation and development but never to use reason in matters of good and evil because we are bound to fail like Adam and Eve did **(Romans 8:7)**. We do not reason God or love, we believe HIM; likewise we must show love even when we find no reason to do so. It's all about faith.

Faith and reason can never be mixed; they are like oil and water! That's why the only people who access the Kingdom of God are like little children who love completely and trust completely and do not seek to reason love or God. Literature on how to stay positive and have a strong will abounds on the market. While being strong-willed and highly motivated are critical to productivity, they are insufficient! Because you can have a ton of will, but you still can't make progress. The book of **Romans 9:16** clarifies: *...so then it is not of him that willeth nor of him that runneth but of God that sheweth mercy.* In other words, mental might and strength belong to a lesser realm in our quest for achievement. To make the most of our lives, and to attain resounding achievement, we must invest spiritually. This brings us to the third and most important dimension of our being-our spirit.

The Spirit is like the computer battery. The battery determines the overall functioning of the computer. Our spirit is the most superior function of our being, capable of controlling the mind and through that, the body. It determines the overall strength of the human and this strength is proportional to the level of attention we give to the spirit. A great man is a spiritual man; a strong man is a spiritual man! The spirit is the place where God relates/fellowships with man, of course, because God is spirit! God keeps us connected to him through our spirit. Through this medium, we receive unadulterated and true inputs from God to keep us in line with His purpose for us. The spirit is where sharp, pure, genuine, gentle, patient, love-oriented, creative ideas are expressed(**Gal 5:25**). It represents the overarching strength of a human being. No doubt the word of God warns that we guard our heart (heart is same as spirit) with diligence for from there come the issues of life (**Proverbs4:23**). Life here stands for fruitfulness, as opposed to dryness or death- with the spirit there is no conflict/doubt/battle. It is the relay station for what is commonly called intuition or inspiration (notice that the word spirit is the root of the term "inspiration"). I fondly call the spirit the "K.O. dimension" because if we allow it to function properly, we would just get a knock out win in every situation like seriously! Jesus Christ, who set precedents on the way we ought to live, taught us how to develop our spirit and to function in it. He stayed with the people, ate with them, interacted with them, but never lost touch with his spirit! His battery never ran low because he always left the people, withdrawing into the hills to charge up by praying and so the spirit of his father always led his thought system, speech and action, hence His victory. The devil has just one intention; for Christians to lose touch with their spirit and consequently their fellowship with God (the Holy Spirit) so that he can drag them to his own battle field, which is the mind, and trounce them there! Dear friends never allow this to happen. Just as the computer battery gets fresh charge from an electrical source to enable the CPU function and get the computer screen ready for the user, so too does the spirit download spiritual charges from God through prayer to overhaul the mind's weakness and give us the right direction every time, every day. In this sense, therefore, prayer is not a moment to present a long list of material needs to God; rather, it's an opportunity to empty our hearts of every evil to take out the trash and to get a fresh in-filling of the Holy Spirit. Prayer is also an opportunity for us to renew our resolve to always let God have HIS way in our lives that he may increase while we decrease. We may not have the luxury of time and opportunity everyday to withdraw from our world of business to rekindle our spirit, but this is the source of our vitality **(Romans8:11)** therefore, we must create time for this. Further, there are smart ways to kick-start a spirit-led life. Start your day by glorifying God, asking for forgiveness for sins of the previous day or the past, meditating on a scripture and asking HIM to lead your day. During the day, allow yourself to have flash reflections for seconds or minutes when you can, to think of what Christ did for you and to count your blessing: sing a song in your heart**(Eph 5:18)**,speak tongues to yourself or overtly as often as you can**(Jude 1:20)**. In the face of every situation, put God first before you act, letting HIM do it for you will produce the best outcome. The miracle about this is that when HE sees your heart and your will to stick to his ways on every count, he swiftly provides you relief and makes the job easier for you**(1Peter3:12)**.The importance of a refreshed spirit can't be overemphasized. It is our source of vitality! No doubt Jesus underscored this in the prayer He taught us: *give us this day our daily bread*-referring to the Holy Ghost's refreshment of our spirit (**Matt6:11**).

The operation of the spirit does not undermine our mental functions but rather enhances them. The mind is a faculty, a gift of God that enables us to analyze and make logical conclusions that help to develop us and our world. What the spirit does is sharpen the mind even better to perfect the ideas that stream from it(**Psalm119:130**). However, and unfortunately too, it is where the devil can penetrate! Therefore, we must restrain its "ungodly excesses" by refreshing our spirits often (ministering to the lord). When we refresh our spirits, we renew our energies, gain confidence in the direction to take, refocus on our dreams and purpose, and rebuild courage to pursue them without giving into the fears and doubts the devil feeds our minds. *They that wait upon the lord shall renew their strength, shall mount up with wings as eagles, run and not be weary, walk and not faint...* (**Is40:31**)this does not mean you sit in the living room like you are waiting for a visitor-remember HE is Spirit and we can only wait upon him with our spirit; always making it ready for HIM to come and dwell and lead us(**John4:25**).When we meditate on his word, pray or fast, we are literarily preparing a seat, waiting for HIM to come reign in our hearts and forge us untiringly to our victory in all we do. Becoming born again is just a step on your success trip. Growing in knowledge and practice of the word of God ensures your victory everyday in this world through Christ Jesus(**2Peter1:1-3**).

Pearls

- ✓ The human being has 3 functional dimensions analogous to the computer: the body like the screen, the mind like the CPU and the spirit like the battery.
- ✓ The human being functions most effectively (faith, purpose-drive, creativity, motivation, direction, progress) when the soul is fine-tuned spiritually.
- ✓ This effectiveness drops when the spirit is less active and the soul depends solely on the mind.

Just like the computer can't function effectively at low battery!
- ✓ A refreshed spirit makes the mind much sharper.
- ✓ The mind allows us to reason and analyze situations, to develop our skill and bring about development in different fields of our choice: science, arts, politics. Let its use be limited to these and to commonsense.
- ✓ In matters of good and evil, the mind is helpless! We must never use it because only faith answers in such matters. We do not reason God, we believe God!
- ✓ Any teaching that seeks to apply reason to issues of faith insults Christ's sacrifice! They are a replication of the encounter between Eve and the serpent in the Garden of Eden which is great displeasure to God.
- ✓ Christ came to set us free from mental slavery.
- ✓ Mental slavery is fueled by two things: fear and pride.

- ✓ Like a fountain of living water is the kingdom of God and is available for all provided they only believe. You do not have to study humanly designed godly literature for several years to qualify, you do not have to be financially sound or highly educated, all you need is to hear the word and believe, not harden your heart(Heb11:4).Isaiah had seen this when he prophesied: *Ho, everyone that thirsteth, come ye to the waters, and he that hath no money; come ye buy, and eat; yea, come, buy wine and milk without money and without price.*(**Is55:1**)
- ✓ When our spirits are strengthened, we become a faith fountain, an impregnable fortress which the devil can't access or defeat!
- ✓ We can charge our spirit by praying both in our understanding and in the Holy Ghost, meditating on and acting on the word of God and fasting.
- ✓ The fiercest battle humans ever fight is the battle of the mind.

- ✓ The devil's greatest wish is that we run out of spiritual charge so he can always drag us to his battle field-the mind–and defeat us there decisively.
- ✓ We need to stay spiritually conscious so we can overhaul the devil's antics that tend to mesmerize our minds.
- ✓ A sharp spirit has a multiplier effect on our mental faculty. Our logical thinking becomes unassailable; like Jesus' was whenever he faced the Pharisees. A spiritual man is like the wind!(**John 3:8**)
- ✓ It is a wonderful thing to train the mind, but training the spirit ramps up our benefits exponentially!
- ✓ A spiritual man understands things faster and much better than a natural man does. You can trust his judgment better than a natural man's.(**1Cor 2:14-15**)
- ✓ Praying in the Holy Ghost is a more powerful refresher! (**1Cor 14:18**)
- ✓ We must seek to refresh our spirits daily.

CHAPTER IV

Why Am I Here?

So God created man in his own image, in the image of God created he him; male and female created he them. And God blessed them, and God said unto them, be fruitful, and multiply and replenish the earth and subdue it and have dominion over the fish of the sea, and over the fowl of the air and over everything that moveth upon the *earth* **Gen1:27-28 (NIV)**

Our existence is not a mere accident. The book of **Jer1:5** tells us: *before you were formed in your mother's womb, I knew you and chose you to be mine...* Out of the 20million sperm cells released in your father's seminal fluid, available to fertilize the egg from your mother, only one was elected to do so. Science is so far inadequate to explain why a particular sperm cell and not the others are elected for this process. Our opinion was not sought for us to be born into this world and there will come a time when we must depart and to a large extent, this does not depend on us! The holy bible teaches us from the opening verses that God created us. When he did create us, he gave us an instruction-it is the fulfillment of that instruction that represents our purpose! A key word that stands out in that instruction is *fruitfulness*. While fruitfulness could be readily interpreted there to mean procreation, it goes beyond mere child bearing. It implicitly indicates productivity! *We are the handiwork of God*...We should see ourselves as stewards in God's vineyard–working hard, busy producing fruits -fruits of love. *You did not choose me, no I chose you and commissioned you to go out and bear fruits, fruits that would last; fruits of love*(**John15:16**)as love is the only thing that would last! All stewards have a duty towards their master! Being stewards to God and therefore to Love, we are all called to love and to serve God, which is reflected by our love and service of one another in our area of stewardship. These two aspects can never be dissociated as John put it; if you don't love your brother whom you see, how can you claim to love God whom you do not see. If we are champions of love, we automatically become champions of life. True success comes from showing love, not the goods and money we amass over time. We are love beings and must act love to maintain our safety, equilibrium and health. This is not negotiable! That is how God designed it. Otherwise, equilibrium is broken and we become dysfunctional and we either get sick in the body, sick in the mind or sick in the spirit irrespective of the money, accolades or recognition we command. So do not be deceived by the outward show some people put up(**1John3:14**). So long as they don't show sincere love, you can consider it as a save-face mechanism, they are actually sick! Not to get this twisted, we need money and material things to live; and we should keep in mind that we can have it beyond our wildest imagination if only we stick to the love principle. God is eternal and because He is eternal, love also is since God is love. Therefore, anyone who sticks to the love principle can be sure that they will echo through eternity for as Paul puts it;*now abides faith, hope and charity and the greatest is charity*(**1Cor13:4**). Just go down the annals of history and pick out those whose actions were driven by love and I will show you love heroes starting with Jesus Christ our Lord and savior! Paul expounds on the qualities of true love in **1Cor 13:4-8.**As we live daily, let these qualities challenge our actions, words and thoughts so that gradually we become true stewards for our master Jesus Christ who will say well done good and faithful servant.

Pearls

- ✓ Fulfilling your purpose is tied to your expression of unconditional love.
- ✓ God has placed in us talents that we must identify for service to others and to his glory.

- ✓ If you are not smart enough to identify your talents and explore them with passion, try exploring unconditional love and you will never be lost!
- ✓ Working in the line of your purpose is God Himself working!
- ✓ Doing anything outside your purpose leads to failure, frustration and rejection.
- ✓ We must identify those things that crave for the most attention within us, those things that we can do readily and for no gain, those things that we are passionate about.
- ✓ Our purpose is like a tree, it has branches meaning we are not tied to one possibility, we are a wellspring of productivity; therefore, our purpose could be updated to spawn several ramifications as life goes on.
- ✓ Love and selflessness are the ideal state of a human being poised for fulfillment!

- ✓ When hatred and selfishness take over, we become dysfunctional either physically, mentally or socially.
- ✓ The true measure of a man is the amount of love he has.
- ✓ A champion of love is a champion of life!
- ✓ When we reach out to others, we are lending to God and He will pay back!(**Proverbs 19:17**).

CHAPTER V

What Is My Area Of Stewardship?

A man's gift maketh room for him and bringeth him before great men... **(Proverbs18:16)**

When we come to terms with who we truly are and why we are here, love beings created to love and serve one another as a means of achieving fulfillment, the next question we should ask is: where do I serve? Determining our area of service is most crucial to attaining our goals and at the same time the most confusing. The buzz of the world and her distractions, economic downturn, inadequate orientation and the gloomy picture painted by the media and ideas from some friends or people instill fear in us, or cloud our minds, making it difficult for us to make the right career choices. Some people have a dream, but do not know the steps to take to get there; others are not even sure what they dream to become, others do not even think it's necessary to work and explore their talents believing that the only reason they are alive is to preach the word of God. Yes you may be called to become a minister of God, but it is no excuse for you to allow your talents to mold away out of disuse! That is an insult to our creator. Some say, "God is in control and will do everything for me, I do not need to bother, there will be a way."Miracles do happen. Yes! But if you fail to put at work the gifts and talents God put inside you before the foundation of the world, you are acting in faithlessness! Faith goes with works always. If you believe God, you must believe in the talents he put inside you and you must be aware that he expects you to use them for his glory. You must make plans, you must be diligent and you must be accountable. When God created every good thing in the Garden of Eden, Adam could just sit still and enjoy but no! God instructed him to tend the garden. Work is a natural call for everyone and we must be diligent at it. In each and everyone, God placed a gift/talent or variety of talents that could be tailored in different careers that we ought to exercise for the service of our neighbor and to the glory of God. He laced this gift-pack with a ribbon. The ribbon stands for unconditional love. He made it in such a way that in order to make the most of life we must unfold the ribbon. It is this unconditional love-ribbon that when unlaced, releases all the goodies that are found within us-then we would have lived our purpose! It takes Christ to do this for us (**2Tim1:9-10**)in other words Christ must be revealed in our hearts first, we must be born again before we can understand unconditional love and then begin to walk with focus in this world! All we need to succeed in life lies only within us. Remember he said *the kingdom of God is within you...* so discovering your purpose in life means unraveling the Kingdom of God within you, demonstrated by a life of unconditional love and the expression of all the treasures hidden within us and living in faith above all possible limitations of this world. When we consider this, we see that we shall live each day happily and victoriously, putting smiles on others faces and glorifying God in the same process. No amount of personal hard work, material possession or fame can afford peace to our soul until Christ shows up!

Looking at the opening scripture, we realize that we are all poised for greatness provided we discover our gifts and begin to make use of them. Now, the world presents myriads of influences that pull and push us in one direction or the other. We find ourselves at the crossroad of influences and are confused as to what steps to take and in what direction: fear, uncertainty, discouragement from friends, a poor business climate, narrow opportunity-frame presented by our country could all compel us to make choices that have nothing to do with our true area of stewardship or gifts God put in us.

All we need do is get up one morning and do a reality check with ourselves; with a cool head, we should try to analyze our innate or learned skills and experiences and match them to a career or set of relevant careers. What am I good at doing? What is that thing that I love doing which I can even do free of charge? Now, we must watch out for that skill that begs for the most attention within us which we can feel so comfortable doing for free-that's an idea of where we should serve!

If you can't do this, ask your friends, teachers or colleagues, odds are they would have an idea. Once you know where you should be, identify what it takes to do this, people you need to meet, what practical steps you need to take to get there. Ask questions addressing them to the right office, right people and stay informed to make sure you are in the right direction. Beyond this reasoned approach lies the inner voice of God's spirit within us which gives us a solid conviction about our true calling. To explore this, we must build strength of spirit through prayer, fasting and meditation on God's word. These will make that voice clearer. If we are unable to still situate ourselves in a particular field, we should still not mind rather, we should continue to act in love at every instant irrespective of where we find ourselves. Love is that searchlight in the dark that will eventually lead us to our specific area of stewardship. Love is our first assignment, walking in the light of love takes us to our second assignment which is the exercise of our gift.

Being established in a specific career does not necessarily make you fulfilled. You may be a great entrepreneur, a wonderful scientist, a statesman, a minister of God or doing just great in a career you chose, but deep down inside, you feel a void that needs to be filled. You may also be someone who has tried to figure out the way forward after trying several things that failed you may have come to the end of yourself and concluded that life is vague and vain! These are symptoms of Christ's absence, an indication you have not unlocked the kingdom of God that lies within you. You may have also been forced by parents or economic hardship to be where you find yourself or you ended up there because 'you had no choice' and you strain at it and are not even effective at it. You can always relocate and start somewhere you truly feel useful and fulfilled. When love guides you to your area of stewardship and you go ahead to exert your duties with love, then you have unraveled the kingdom of God within you and you have found your purpose! However, purpose never ends. Like a seed, it grows. In that field where you are called, you must be productive; you must upgrade and use the resources, information at your disposal to expand that purpose for the greatest possible impact in your world. Purpose is ever-growing and keeps developing as the need to serve increases and I bet you there will always be some service to render somewhere until we die. We were born to serve.

Only the word of God can guarantee this (**Joshua 1:8, Psalm1:2-3**)*cut off from me you can do nothing*(-**John15:5, Phil 4:13**).The Kingdom of God is not meat and drink but of joy, peace and righteousness in the Holy Ghost. The Kingdom of God has a language, one and only one language: LOVE-*he who abides in love abides in God and God in him*. It is this deep love of God that gives us the ability to live with others in harmony, work selflessly and walk righteously. Love is subtle and unassuming but carries a potent force for change in any situation! It is the relentless pursuit of love that ultimately takes us to where we had to be in life.

Pearls

- ✓ The kingdom of God is within us.

- ✓ The kingdom of God is a system of love.
- ✓ Belief in and quest for Jesus Christ in the word of God makes that love system obvious to us.
- ✓ Discovering our purpose means unraveling the kingdom of God that is within us.
- ✓ Expressing unconditional love everyday is the searchlight that reveals to us our area of stewardship.
- ✓ If you are not sure of the career you want to get into, just stick to your primary assignment-love! And you will never be lost.
- ✓ Jesus Christ is the light of life!
- ✓ Once we have the light, we can clearly see everything in this world as it really is.
- ✓ Love is the driving force behind any true and worthy purpose.
- ✓ Without an encounter with true Love-Jesus Christ of Nazareth–it is impossible to discover and live your purpose. *Cut off from me you can do nothing. He is the author and finisher of our faith.*

- ✓ Allow the love of what you want to do be the primary criterion for selecting your career.
- ✓ When you are doing what your heart leads you to do and are doing it with love, God Himself is at work!
- ✓ Never settle for what you truly never wanted to do-you will never be happy! Keep challenging yourself until you are where you feel fulfilled.
- ✓ Purpose is ever growing, ever developing and reaches out to others. Picture the seed that becomes a tree, the tree that becomes shelter for birds...
- ✓ Once in the line of your purpose, there is no limit to the things you can do.
- ✓ When you find joy, peace and righteousness (ability and willingness to persistently do right) in what you do, then you are on the right track.

CHAPTER VI

Open Up The Limits

But whosoever drinketh of the water that I shall give him shall never thirst; but the water that I shall give him shall be in him a well of water springing up into everlasting life (**John 4:14**)

There is actually no limit to what we can achieve in our lifetime. Jesus had this in mind when he told his disciples: *out of your belly shall flow springs of living water...* Recognize that water symbolizes life and freshness-living water at that! It is a boundless sea of possibilities that we can achieve and also deliver to others once our intention is love. It also indicates how much we could bless this world as many will come to this fountain of pure love, inspiration. Setting out with the love of God is the only necessary condition for this. *I came that you may have life and have it more abundantly.* (**John 10:10**)-This underscores the idea of boundlessness. Abundant life is the life of God, the life that gives life, the life that is rooted in love, the life that blesses, the life that restores, and the life that knows no limits. God's love is all about outreach. There is no blind end rather there is a continuous outpouring from the source which we extend to others and which they must in turn extend to others. I very much think of eternal life as one that has a multiplier effect. There is always a compulsion to share it! With his grace, it ripples to keep growing and achieving more.

Jesus illustrated this in his teachings and parables. He said the kingdom of God is like a mustard seed that is planted, grows into a tree and then birds come and perch on its branches for shade. Here the idea of productivity, development and outreach are also being highlighted. The seed that grows into a tree, a tree with several branches, branches that provide shade for birds!(**1Peter 1:23 Matt 5**)

When we encounter stress and difficulty in our fields of work, we can always draw encouragement from the word of God which, by the way, should be our reference and our manual.

You are more than conquerors! **(1John 5:4)**, an over-comer(**1John4:4**).Having great assurance that Christ who sees the end from the beginning has already taken care of the stress and we shall emerge successful at the end of the day.

Yes, *I can do all things through Christ which strengtheneth me,* but this doesn't mean you should venture into just anything which is not in line with your in-born or learned abilities. While it is important to realize that it is Christ's ability working in us that registers our victory in any endeavor we choose, we must recognize that we have the ultimate responsibility to steer Christ's ability in us in the direction that is most suitable for our personality and skills. Whichever fields our strengths seem to be oriented, let's maximize God's grace and spirit in these areas so we can make the most out of these fields. The kingdom of God is a small step we take that triggers a tremendous measure of productivity with no limits to what we can achieve. It only takes faith! *The kingdom of God is like a woman who mixes three measures of flour with one measure of leaven and the whole bowl leavens.* Jesus Christ has charted the course already for us**(Eph2:10)**. When we received him in faith, he unlocked all the potentialities within us. He is that leaven that is mixed with three measures of flour that leavens the whole bowl. Therefore, all we need do is take a bold step of faith and to venture into the fields of our endeavor, keeping love on our minds always and we shall realize limitless success**(Psalm 1, Joshua 1:8)**.

- ✓ Abundant life is the God kind of life, it is the life rooted in love, it is the life that gives life, and it knows no limits.
- ✓ As children of God, we are merely a channel of God's love.

CHAPTER VII

Run With The Vision

And the Lord answered me, and said Write the vision, and make it plain on tables, that he may run that readeth it. (**Hab2:2**)

If success has to be realized in any way, time must be factored in. Time is one big regulator. It helps us evaluate our performance, serves as a reality check and helps to remind us of where we are lagging and where work needs to be done. In fact, it helps us fan the flames of our vision and move closer everyday to achieving it. It judges us. Time is a precious gift to us. When we waste time mindlessly, we never get it back. Time cumulatively considered represents our lifetime. When we waste time, we waste our lives. Trying to understand who we are and our role in the world adds more value to our lives as we would become better time managers and shall see ourselves as stewards from whom God expects results and we would be ultimately efficient in our dealings. The activities of the world, the media, habits, friends, all crave for attention and we easily get swallowed by these things that we do not sit for a while to contemplate our purpose and time just passes. We must manage our time wisely and learn to not procrastinate. We must spend more time doing things that bring us closer to our dreams, and with people who bring us closer to those dreams. We must be alert and wage a constant war on distractions!...*do not be ignorant of the devices of the enemy*... the bible warns us. Distractions are a device of the enemy because they steal our time, derail us from the line of our purpose and as a result render us unproductive contrary to the will of God.

A distraction is anything you spend more time on than on your purpose per 24hr period. Distractions are usually alluring and tend to be addictive. They usually creep into our minds gradually and before we know it, they have taken over us! They may take a surprising variety of forms: alcohol, TV, movies, music, Facebook, Twitter, blogs, food, romance novels, video games, pornography, fashion, drugs, mindless chatting. Appreciating the toll these distractions have on your life may be the first step to win your war on them. Identify your distractions, calculate the time spent on them each day and estimate how many years that may represent over a 50year period; you will be shocked at how many years of your precious life you are actively working on throwing down the drain! Let's do a little math. Say you spend approximately 4hours (maybe you spend more) on your distraction or set of distractions daily that means $4/24=1/6^{th}$ of your day. That sounds little, but say you have to live for 50years more; that gives us $1/6 \times 50 = 8.3$years about 8 and half years you are actively working on wasting! Now, you are likely to defend yourself by saying your distractions do not necessarily feature on your daily programs-well you may be right, but odds are that they do, given their nature. Even if you are right, that may just nibble a little fraction off the 8.3years! You may still be staring at seven whole years of your life potentially vanishing unproductive! That's no joke pal!!It took some people less than 7years of diligence to be settled for life. After recognizing this grim fact, you can then go on your knees to pray and study the word of God, denouncing each distraction by name and resolving to quit. You may have to do this several times, but that's okay. You could also seek help from a friend with more spiritual maturity; *iron sharpeneth iron*(**Proverbs27:17**).

David prayed a prayer*: teach me Lord to number my days that I may apply my heart unto wisdom.* It is very important for us to plan our lives, to set a timeline for accomplishing various goals we set for ourselves in the line of our purpose. The more we plan our time, the wiser we become and we accomplish our goals with high efficiency. You could develop a long-term plan, for say 5years or 10years from now. Tell yourself where you want to be and what you wish to see accomplished by then. Now you can split this into a short-term plan, say for the year and you could further split this to come up with a quarterly plan. The next thing is to discipline yourself against procrastination and to stick to your timeline religiously. Through such discipline, the fruits of your efforts will appear and you shall flourish. After setting up such discipline and you still do not accomplish a goal at a planned time, you do not have to freak out. God has a reason why and remember we make our plans, but He has the final word**(Proverbs 16:9)** and whatever it turns out to be, it's in our best interest. However, you must do your part by making the plans and executing them in the first place.

All we have in a day is 24hrs. We can never have an extra minute added to this. If we must improve our output, our only option is to modify our activity schedule. Making every moment count is difficult because our energy levels fluctuate and distractions are real and they abound. The best way forward is to make the most use of the moments you feel energetic and fresh and to avoid any distractions at this time. Experience has proven that the early hours of a day are critical for human productivity (be it the mind or the body). Prioritizing your daily goals and fitting the most important ones within the first six hours of the day can speed your achievement. A good rule of thumb would be completing your most crucial tasks before the sun goes up! The rest of the day could be reserved for less tasking activities. This is in no way a hard and fast rule, just a suggestion that has proven to be helpful for many people. You know best what works for you; all you need do is identify what time of the day you experience peak productivity and place your most important tasks here- as long as you do not allow a distraction to steal your peak productivity period, you are still good. Having an adequate night's rest of about 7-8hours and rising early are vital habits to productivity. Exercise, eating a healthy diet and drinking enough water keep you smart and boost your output.

CHAPTER VIII

Effort Alone Is Insufficient... Faith Is A Must!

Trust in the Lord with all thine heart; and lean not unto thine own understanding.(**Proverbs3:5**)

Hard work is an age-old value. It is arguably the most essential contributor to the success of any human endeavor. There is no doubt about the place of diligence in the realization of our achievement and development. The book of proverbs corroborates; *seest thou a man diligent in his business? he shall stand before kings*. Through daily efforts of work, we earn our salaries, cater for others, realize major projects, and make advancement in our academic, professional, family and social lives. While there is no gainsaying to the invaluable merits of diligence, it leaves something to be considered the key to success.

There comes a time when we know we have put in our most, but we still feel far from what we believe we reasonably deserve. We yet try another route and another and another yet we lurk head-on with obstacles. This happens to every human being at some point; everything seems to come to a standstill and we feel we have reached the end of the road with no glimmer of hope in the distant horizon! This feeling comes to us because we envision our human efforts as the unique ingredient to bring progress in our lives, but this is false! If we are not born again, we must become to start with; that is a basic and essential step we MUST make(see chapter II). Now if we are, we must realize that we stewards who do not have the last word on where we should be or how things should turn out. Then can we begin to appreciate faith in God as a more substantial aspect of our journey through life. In this regard, we are expected to leave everything to God, not 'some things'. We hold on to nothing, sit back and just watch him fight our battles. The Psalmist says in **Psalm 25:1***the Lord is my shepherd I shall not want*. As children of God, that is what we are to Jesus Christ-we can only be led to pasture. We do not choose our pasture and we do not choose the rivers from which to drink. All we need to know is that our shepherd is a good shepherd and therefore we trust that He will take us to what we need to develop our lives and to enjoy true fulfillment. There is never a dry land for a man of faith and once a man pleases God,(remember that only faith pleases God) even his enemies will be at peace with him **(Proverbs16:7)**.When we talk faith, the phrase "bad news" ceases to exist in our dictionaries. Whatever the world thinks and knows is bad for us is still good for us**(Romans 8:28)**. This is because it is not only our goals that matter to God, but also the faith-building processes it takes to reach those goals. Let's never forget that we are in a love relationship with our father the moment we repent, so He takes much delight in that relationship and wants us to abide in him. He realizes however that we may make some bad choices at times that make us stray from him, so he double-checks to ensure that we always return home like sheep to the fold. Never weep, never regret when you feel you are in an unfortunate situation, rather, just say "thank you Lord" and be grateful that he has given you another chance to rest in his bosom, to stay in fellowship with the Holy Spirit; for in effect, that is the essence of our "mishaps", they are a double-check for our fellowship with the Holy Ghost. We must always fall back.

Faith indeed empowers us in times of despair, realigns our thought system, rejuvenates our resolve and dispels the cloud of frustration, self-blame and depression that loom over us when we reach that end of the road. In fact, faith is everything for us: our lives, our cares, our sure source of strength.

It is important to note that there is a sharp disparity between one who has received Christ and one who has not with regards to difficulty and pain. For an unsaved man, the devil is able to cause damage up to and including death! For he who has received Christ, all the devil does is help him build his faith and even when he passes on, his end will be an expected one(**Jer 29:11**).

Faith in God ensures our victory in every difficult circumstance and the first step of faith is humbling oneself under the mighty hand of God-namely through repentance.

Jesus recounted a parable to his friends at a certain time. It was about hard-work and reward. Stewards were hired for a certain task and they came at different times and consequently they put in varying hours for the job. However when the time for reward came, they all received the same prize. The ones who had put in more hours became indignant about the reward their counterparts had received. Notice that they did not ask for more reward, but were simply displeased that others who had not worked as hard received the same amount as they.This is typical of a natural man's behavior, always competing, comparing and wishing to be more than the others. Unfortunately or fortunately, that's not how it works in God's system! The amount of work we do is no indicator of our rewards; love matters most- the scripture says: *promotion cometh neither from the east, nor from the west, nor from the south but God is the*

Judge of all; he putteth down one, and setteth up another **(Psalms75:6-7)**. We must not look at others but just discharge our assignments with unconditional love and allow God almighty to handle the rewarding. Love does not compare with others **(1Cor 13:4-8)**. We must not compare ourselves with others; if anything, we should esteem ourselves lower than others **(Phil 2:3)**. Humble yourself and you shall be exalted.

CHAPTER IX

Communicate Adequately and Wisely

Ask and it shall be given you; seek, and ye shall find, knock and it shall be opened unto you…(**Matt7:7**)

Someone once said that the difference between our present and our future is information. Interpreting along those lines we can infer that the more informed we are, the better prepared we are to meet our future and the greater the odds that we succeed. Everything around us is information in its right: the news, the weather, people, the market, the church, and workplace. Information greases the rails of our effort, enables us to strategize, and helps us to be proactive. Information opens up our horizons of possibilities; information boosts our self-esteem and confidence. Information on its own is inadequate; the quality of information and what we do with it makes the difference. This chapter will dwell more on how to obtain valued information and winning communication skills rather than what we do with information. If our future has to be worth reckoning with, we need the right information. Now, who can be a better source of information than the Holy Spirit Himself? The bible tells us that the Holy Spirit will teach us all things!**(John 2:27)** The bible tells us again that He searches all things, the deep things, even the deep things of God**(Romans8:24-26)**,so we are not completely left in the dark! No doubt the opening verse continues: *how much more will your heavenly father give good things to those who ask him.* **Matt7:7-10)**. Good things refer to the Holy Spirit who is the source of all good things, the express person of God Himself in our daily life. He is the director, comforter and much more. God is aware of the confusion that overwhelm his children and the fears and drudgeries of this world, so He devised a means to strengthen us and keep us on track; that is the soft bidding of his voice in our hearts. This pre-set director who has been there from the time we were conceived could be clouded by our own ways; when we follow our own designs contrary to God's will, the voice becomes gradually fainter and over time, our minds are reduced to a mist of confusion, which does not glorify God. No doubt he says: *all have sinned and fall short of the glory of God*.

So, to restore God's glory in our lives, we need to refresh that voice and become more sensitive to it. He needs us to return to the fold in true repentance, in other words be born again! This is the first step to take. When this is done in sincerity, we must go further to study the word of God regularly because the word of God is the spirit of God(**John 6:63**). The more of it we know and put into practice, the more sensitive we become to the soft voice within us and consequently we would make choices that would bring us true fulfillment in life.

Obviously, God uses several ways to get a message across to us. Friends and parents advise us, circumstances teach us, ministers of God sermonize. While it's a good thing to listen and to allow ourselves to consider every piece of advice we receive, we must make a background check with the holy spirit- in other words we must follow our hearts ultimately!

Commonsense and our ability to make reasoned inferences is another strength we are blessed with. Every day, we interact with the world and we make different decisions: at work, at home, in the church and anywhere else we get to interact. Commonsense comes in as an essential tool in all this and we must use it. If you are abreast with what the word of God says, you will make many decisions with confidence because the spirit of God within you will witness to you the truth. If however in your commonsense decisions you still feel doubtful and confused, it is time for you to go back to the word and study it so that you can make decisions with relative ease because God's word is his spirit and it brings light or better still clarifies issues and gives you good results**(1Tim4:15, Psalms119:130)**.

The benefits of communication cannot be overstated. Communication is the cornerstone for success in any human endeavor whatsoever! In governments, business organizations, relationship/marriage, family, politics .This stems from the fundamental truth that this world is peopled by different souls with varied reasoning patterns, IQs, backgrounds, experiences, skills and genetic make-up. Even when we come from the same family there are varieties and by virtue of different exposures we get. Therefore to be able to trace your path to your goals, you must be ready to deal with differences; differences in ideas, differences in perceptions, differences in faces and you can't do this without being able to communicate effectively. Never assume anything; ask questions when in doubt. Communication is what levels you with others, to drive your dreams through in any uncomfortable and tortuous situation. It must be done wisely for three reasons; firstly, communication helps us to explore our world to our advantage, guiding us to fish out those people, skills, and resources that we need to accomplish our goals. Proper communication smoothes out any rough edges in relationships keeps you on the same page with your partner or associate, or colleague. Lastly, communication fosters unity and progress **(Psalm 133:1)**.

Do not use harmful words in talking, use only helpful words, the type that build up the spirit(**Eph 4:29**).We must avoid being aggressive with our points of view and not unnecessarily submissive as well! Being assertive and considerate strikes the balance. Not everyone will agree with you on your way to fulfilling your vision, but that is okay! For Christ himself faced a stiff opposition, yet he overcame and he assured us we will overcome in a like manner so never ever give up on your God-given vision!

Pearls

- ✓ The Holy Spirit, that soft voice within you, should be your first informant and director.
- ✓ Reasoning and commonsense should be subject to spiritual discernment(**Proverbs 3:5-6,Psalm 119:105**)
- ✓ Take a bold step and ask questions when you are in doubt of anything and do your research on whatever information you believe can help you achieve your goals.(**Matt7:7**)

- ✓ The words you speak are like the vehicles that transport you into your future; good or bad. **(Proverbs 18:21)**
- ✓ As a child of God, your words are sanctified; therefore, speak words of faith, love and hope. In short, speak life!
- ✓ Let your words build others and not destroy them instead.
- ✓ When your communication is sufficient and love-supervised, your path to achievement is paved.
- ✓ Communication sets the stage for any human progress whether individual or collective.

CHAPTER X

Relax...Shine A Smile!

...do not grieve for the joy of the Lord is your strength
Neh 8:10 (NIV)

Joy is a central quality of anyone who has truly met Christ; someone who loves unconditionally. It is their default mode because of the Holy Spirit that dwells in them. In our world today, joy is a rare asset! We can count on the fingers of one hand people we know that are truly happy. Some put up appearances but experience pain deep inside. Our world is a hurting one. Some try to cope with the hurt by resorting to alcohol, engaging in unhealthy relationships, yet others succumb to depression and some others even dare to take away their lives and some succeed to do so. It's a cold world: economic hardship, social conflicts, unmet career expectations, poor health, death of a loved one, and undue pressures from work-the list of these joy-stealers is unending. In the midst of all these, a man whose life is built on Christ holds firm, enjoys inner peace and is capable of even putting a smile on others' faces; *..you will be like the man who built his house on solid rock* **Matt 7:24-25 (NIV)**. It is hard to comprehend the joy and peace which the Holy Spirit brings to a soul, but when we look at what the word of God says, we begin to understand that whatever comes our way that can potentially cause us stress is already taken care of. This is the confidence that we must never part with; that he will never abandon us or forsake us, even in the midst of the storm **(Is 43:1-3, Heb13:5).** *Ye are of God little children and have overcome them because greater is he that is in you than he that is in the world.* **(1John4:4).** A comforting peace and joy automatically fill our hearts once we know we already have the victory because of Christ who dwells in us **(1Cor15:57)**. There is joy in faith, there is peace in faith. Another reason why one who loves unconditionally experiences unstoppable joy is because love chases fear away and replaces it with an atmosphere of peace, joy, hope and strength. *There is no fear in love but perfect love casteth out fear; for fear hath torments. He that feareth is not made perfect in love.*(**1John4:18**).

Remember the Holy Spirit is our comforter(**John 16:13**). When our activities did not go as planned; when we failed to reach the profit margin of our daily business, it's no reason for us to get depressed. We can still relax knowing that the master planner will put everything in place. Once you accept as a Christian that God is in charge of your life and not you, you become less anxious and truly enjoy your walk with him. Just do your best and leave the rest to Him. *Be anxious for nothing but through prayer with supplication and thanksgiving, make your request known unto God and the peace of the Lord that surpasseth all understanding shall guard your hearts and mind through Christ Jesus.*(**Phil 4:6**).This should be the thought that must start you up for the day and remain with you through the end. God understands our worries more than we do. After leaving everything in God's hands, we must maintain our peace by feeding on the word because it is the word that heals**(Psalm 107:20)**; it is the word that strengthens. When you truly trust God, there is never an unfortunate situation-everything turns out just great. The devil likes it when we complain, moan and grieve over issues; he uses this to gradually sink people into depression. Once we catch ourselves complaining, we should remember past situations in our lives in which God saw us through. Also we must remember that faith in God comes by hearing HIS word, therefore, we must take every opportunity to listen to or study his word and so build our faith**(Romans10:17)** to understand that even our present situation is in total control by him. When a situation tempts you to despair, just remember to customize this striking and comforting statement king David made: *since I was young until now I have never seen the righteous forsaken nor his children beg for bread*. **Psalm37:25 (NIV).** Besides this wholesome panacea of faith and prayer, an extra dose of strength, joy and inner peace can be reaped from certain activities most people tend to take for granted. These include, but are not limited to, having a balanced diet; making sure to include lots of fruits and veggies, drinking enough water, moderate intensity aerobic exercise(jogging, swimming, biking, brisk walking, gardening), singing,and listening to music(soft melodic worship).

Summary

S.T.A.R.T.S

S-Strategize: Open up your spirit to Christ: acknowledge your guilt and sincerely make amends with Him and with men, pursue a Christ-conscious attitude by allowing his teachings(which you should study of course) to influence your life and always acknowledge him as Lord of your life-congratulations you are born again! Continuing in this Christ-conscious attitude progressively smothers your ego, heightens your love for others, and unlocks the treasures of true fulfillment in your daily life. Seek the good in every situation. Know your strengths/talents and build a career around them. If you can't identify them, it's okay! – Only, continue to live a love-led life and you will never be a loser!

T-Tenacious: Pursue your dreams earnestly and know you are a winner come what may! Memorize faith boosting scriptures and let them be your shield against the fear, discouragement and faithlessness the world around you breeds. Life means living in faith on earth! So you must have that in mind and soldier on no matter the weather.

A-Act now: Time is life. If you waste time, you waste your life! Spend more time around people and activities that get your dreams further down the road. Whatever you think of doing, go ahead and start at once. Be wary of distractions! They come in different guises and insidiously too. You may fall prey, but it's okay Just "press reset"! This means you should prayerfully denounce them and make up your mind to go a day or two without them. When you do so, you would realize how precious your time is and you will be amazed at how productive you become. You may not get it right the first time, so you can press reset again and again-that's still okay!**(1Tim4:15, 18)**Seeking advice and counseling from a partner can be very rewarding as well. Know your peak productivity

Summary

period of the day and program your most important tasks here(it's the early hours of the day for most people). Do not allow any distraction during your peak productivity period. View your day's activities as made up of "Ds" duty or distraction. Strive to accomplish more of the first "D" than the second.

R-Ritualize: You have three obligatory rituals daily: prayer, working on your goals and showing love. Do not let one day pass by without fulfilling these fundamentals. On a given day, it's possible you miss out on prayer and even more likely you miss out on your goals, but as for showing love, get obsessed with this one, never miss it! 24hours provide you several opportunities to do so. It is the greatest and will always get you back on track-guaranteed 100%!! But remember that prayer molds your personality and enables you to show love with minimal effort.

T- Talk your way to your dreams: Communicate wisely and sufficiently. Ask questions when in doubt. Do not be aggressive or unnecessarily submissive, but rather be assertive. Silence may be the best option at times. Do not use harmful words in talking, but use edifying words instead. Remember that words make or mar your life so talk wisely. Above all else, pronounce words of blessing on your life and your environment, not negative or cursing words. Words build your life, words build your future. Never stop talking positively about your future prospects. Remember that speaking the word of God into your dream is the most potent factor in realizing the dream. There are specific verses that suit particular life events, so you must make sure to locate and speak the appropriate word into the appropriate situation.

S-Smile: Smile at the least opportunity; it greases the rails of work and keeps you healthy. Recognize the fun in everyday life and laugh hard! Exercise, music, sleep, group activities, a healthy diet and a healthy relationship/marriage are just as worthy. Above all else, relax in the awareness that God is in control of your life and will never abandon or forsake you. No matter how hard you work, keep in mind that your faith in God is more critical in determining your achievement and fulfillment in life, so let God be God and you remain his subject. We could all say like Paul: *Not that we are sufficient of ourselves to think anything of ourselves, our sufficiency is of Christ.***(2Cor3:5)**

Food for thought

Someone asked me what I considered success to be. This is what I had to say;

"Success is not an end, success is not a means, to some people it turns out to be a meaningless end, but in truth, it is an endless means. The 'means' here stands for the Kingdom of God and the endlessness of the means implies that the fulfillment that accrues to it is eternal!" The good news is that we can all access this 'means' because the kingdom of God is within us.

Prayer

Lord Jesus, I come to you this day with all my heart, with all my soul, with all my might! I know you came from heaven, walked the earth and were crucified for my sins. Deliver me this day from the yoke of the enemy, wash me with your precious blood and fill me with your spirit. Reveal into my heart the mystery of the Kingdom of God. Thank you, Jesus for saving my soul. Amen

www.ingramcontent.com/pod-product-compliance
Ingram Content Group UK Ltd.
Pitfield, Milton Keynes, MK11 3LW, UK
UKHW041946230426
12048UKWH00008B/160